CLEVELAND ELEMENTARY SCHOOL

NORTH VANCOUVER, B.C.

CLEVELAND ELEMENTARY SCHOOL

NORTH VANCOUVER, B.C.

D0568000

SCIENCE FILES

materials

TEXTILES

Please visit our web site at: www.garethstevens.com
For a free color catalog describing Gareth Stevens Publishing's
list of high-quality books and multimedia programs,
call 1-800-542-2595 or fax your request to (414) 332-3567.

Library of Congress Cataloging-in-Publication Data

Parker, Steve.
    Textiles / by Steve Parker. — North American ed.
        p. cm. — (Science files. Materials)
    Includes bibliographical references and index.
    Summary: Discusses various natural and artificial fibers that are used to produce cloth,
  and examines processes used to transform those fibers into clothing, household items, and
  technological devices.
    ISBN 0-8368-3086-5 (lib. bdg.)
    1. Textile fabrics—Juvenile literature. [1. Textiles. 2. Fibers.] I. Title.
  TS1446.P37   2002
  677—dc21   2001054229

This North American edition first published in 2002 by
Gareth Stevens Publishing
A World Almanac Education Group Company
330 West Olive Street, Suite 100
Milwaukee, WI 53212 USA

Original edition © 2001 by David West Children's Books. First published in Great Britain
in 2001 by Heinemann Library, Halley Court, Jordan Hill, Oxford OX2 8EJ, a division of Reed
Educational and Professional Publishing Limited. This U.S. edition © 2002 by Gareth Stevens, Inc.
Additional end matter © 2002 by Gareth Stevens, Inc.

David West Editor: James Pickering
David West Designers: Rob Shone, Fiona Thorne, David West
Picture Research: Carrie Haines
Gareth Stevens Editor: Alan Wachtel
Gareth Stevens Designer and Cover Design: Katherine A. Goedheer

Photo Credits:
Abbreviations: (t) top, (m) middle, (b) bottom, (l) left, (r) right

Ardea London Ltd.: François Gohier (13tr); Nick Gordon (12tr); Richard Waller (10bl, 10tr, 10–11);
Wardene Weisser (13br, 14bl).
British Camel Association: Peter Jeffries (13tl).
Culture Pavilion: 19bm, 19br.
DuPont: 28bl.
Mary Evans Picture Library: 5tr, 7r, 15tr, 16tr, 23br.
Robert Harding Picture Library: 13mr, 18bl, 26t; G & P Corrigan (15br); Jeff Greenberg (8bl);
J. Legate (29tr); Duncan Maxwell (9tr); Occidor Ltd. (14br, 15bl); Schuster (9tl); Bildagentur Schuster
(5b, 29b); Bildagentur Schuster/Bramaz (23t); Bildagentur Schuster/Eckstein (6l); Charlie Westerman
(cover [bl], 3, 21r); J.H.C. Wilson (20t); Adam Woolfit (11bl).
Ann Ronan Picture Library: 11br, 14tr, 22t, 27tr.
Science Photo Library: Jack K. Clark/Agstock (9bl); Debra Ferguson/Agstock (16l inset); John Eastcott
& Yva Momatiuk (6–7); Carlos Munoz-Yague/Eurelios (9br); Philippe Plailly/Eurelios (11tr).
Rosenfeld Images Ltd. (Cover [tl], 4b, 28m); Ed Young (Cover [br], 8tr).
Spectrum Colour Library: M. Ryan (11tl); Cover [bm], 12bl, 21tl.

Printed in the United States of America

1 2 3 4 5 6 7 8 9 06 05 04 03 02

SCIENCE FILES

materials

TEXTILES

Steve Parker

Gareth Stevens Publishing
A WORLD ALMANAC EDUCATION GROUP COMPANY

CONTENTS

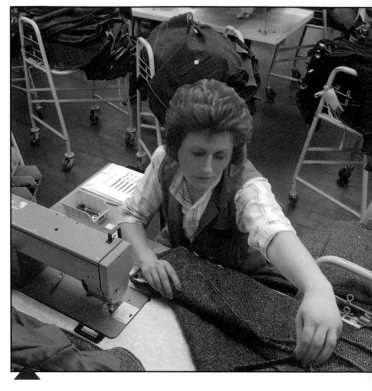

Many items of clothing are still cut out and stitched together by skilled workers rather than by machines. The exact shape of the garment can be varied to suit the type of cloth and the way it stretches over or drapes from the body.

INTRODUCTION

Long ago, someone felt cold and made the first clothes. The first items of clothing were probably cloaks of furry animal skins. By about 7,000 years ago, people were weaving together animal hairs or strands of plant fibers to make sheets of cloth — the earliest textiles. Today, textiles are a huge world industry. Cloths, fabrics, and materials are not only used to cover our bodies and keep us warm. They are made into curtains, rugs, seat and furniture covers and are also used in planes, cars, high-tech sports gear, tires, and spacecraft. They are almost everywhere!

Spinning and weaving were once done by hand. Machines like this power loom made the work go much faster.

◄ *The past one hundred years have seen the invention of many artificial (man-made) fibers, such as nylon, acrylic, and polyester.*

◄ *Artificial fibers make great fabrics for sports clothing. They are lightweight, stretchy, smooth, and comfortable.*

5

NATURAL FIBERS

Textiles are made from fibers, or filaments, that are long, thin, and flexible. Natural fibers come from plants and animals. Flax, cotton, wool, and silk are natural types of fibers that have been used since ancient times.

FIBER FEATURES

Fibers for textiles should be flexible so that they can bend for weaving or similar processes. The fibers should be long and strong so the textile does not fall apart or tear too easily. And they also should be long-lasting so the items made from them do not rot away or fall apart.

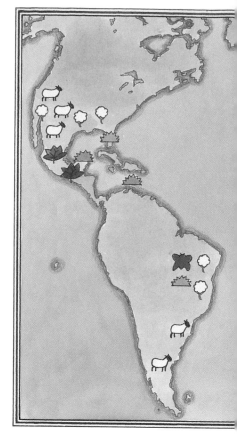

Flax (left) was a very common fiber used to make linen cloth, but in the 1800s, cotton became more popular.

Different breeds of sheep (below) provide wool with various features.

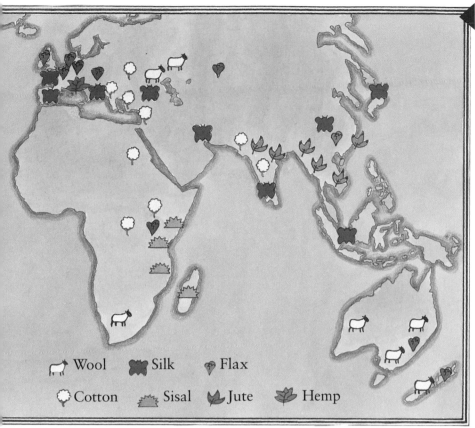

Wool   Silk   Flax

Cotton   Sisal   Jute   Hemp

Each region of the world produces different natural fibers that depend partly on which plants grow in its climate and which animals live there. The fibers also depend on the customs and traditions of the people. In China, the origin of silk was kept secret until silkworms were smuggled to the Middle East in 552 B.C.

FACTS FROM THE PAST

Most natural fibers are stretched out and twisted together to make long lengths of ropelike yarn or thread. This craft is known as spinning. In Ancient Greece, spinning was a relaxing pastime for rich ladies.

Ancient Greek woman spinning

MORE FIBER FEATURES

The fibers used for textiles also have special features that they pass on to the fabric made from them. Silk is very smooth and slippery. Because it is curly and springy, sheep's wool traps air between the fibers for warmth. Much thicker, stronger natural fibers from certain plants are used for making string, twine, rope, and mats.

COTTON AND FLAX

In the textile industry, the most common natural fiber is cotton. Most of the T-shirts, socks, pants, underwear, and towels in the world begin as cotton plants.

HAIRY SEEDPODS

Cotton fibers come from the part of the cotton plant called the boll, or seed head. Cotton bolls are white and fluffy with fibers that are 3/4 to almost 1 1/4 inches (2 to 3 centimeters) long. Since the useful cotton fibers, also known as lint, are mixed up with the plant's seeds, the fibers must be separated from the seeds by a process called ginning.

Cotton plants take 4–6 months to produce ripe bolls, which are picked by machines.

GINNING COTTON

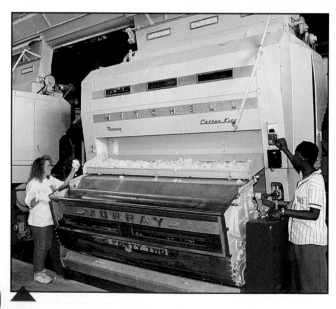

Gins separate fibers from seeds.

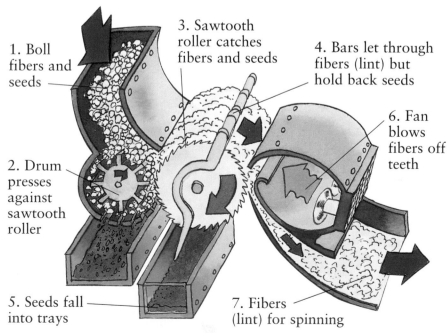

1. Boll fibers and seeds

2. Drum presses against sawtooth roller

3. Sawtooth roller catches fibers and seeds

4. Bars let through fibers (lint) but hold back seeds

5. Seeds fall into trays

6. Fan blows fibers off teeth

7. Fibers (lint) for spinning

Flax plants are grown for the long fibers in their stems and also for their seeds. The seeds are squashed, or pressed, to release their oil, known as linseed oil.

After drying, flax stems are beaten and scraped, or scutched, to loosen the long fibers within the stems.

FLAX

Flax fibers come from the flax plant's stalk, or stem. The plants are harvested by hand or by machine. The stalks are retted, or soaked in water, for several days or weeks. After they dry, they are beaten and scraped, and then hackled, or combed, to release and smooth the fibers.

Bales of ginned cotton fibers, ready for spinning

The first cotton gin was invented by Eli Whitney in 1793–1794. The cotton gin separates fibers from seeds and other bits of the boll. It also helps clean and comb the fibers, which are packed into bales. Cottonseeds are used for vegetable oils, margarines, soaps, and animal foods.

IDEAS FOR THE FUTURE

The fibers in cotton bolls are white. One day, however, they may be any color you wish. Cotton plants might be changed by genetic modification. This would reduce the need to dye, or color, the fibers later.

Could cotton grow colored?

OTHER PLANT FIBERS

Several kinds of plants have strong, stringy fibers used for making textiles. The fibers of these plants are removed by various methods, such as shaking, soaking, and scraping, similar to how fibers are released from flax plants (*see page 9*).

JUTE AND SISAL

Jute is a tall plant that grows over 11 feet (3.5 meters) high. Jute fibers come from under its barklike skin. Since they are long, thick, and coarse, they are used to make bags, ropes, carpet backs, and linings. Sisal fibers come from the sisal plant's leaves. They are also coarse and are used for ropes, brushes, and rough cloth.

Each leaf of the sisal plant contains more than 1,000 fibers, each up to 5 feet (1.5 m) long, that are used for making rope.

Jute is grown mainly in India and nearby countries. Its stems are soaked in water, dried, and crushed to loosen and separate the fibers.

Jute is taken by boat to the spinning factory. Its fibers are fairly weak and brittle, and they do not hold dyes well.

Kapok bushes grow to several yards (m) high.

About 8 feet (2.5 m) long, hemps fibers are tough and long-lasting. They are dried and removed like flax fibers.

KAPOK AND HEMP

The light, fine, fluffy fibers of kapok are found on the tree's seedpods. They are used for stuffing and padding. Hemp fibers come from the hemp plant's stem. Their main uses include making bags, ropes, rough canvas, and sack material.

Most fibers are spun, or twisted, into yarn or thread.

This is a jute-spinning factory.

FACTS FROM THE PAST

Hemp resists water and rotting. It was made into hammocks, ropes, strings, and cords for old sailing ships. Today, like many other natural fibers, hemp has been mostly replaced by stronger artificial fibers.

Hauling with a hemp rope

11

WOOL

Wool is the soft, wavy hair of sheep. It is the most common animal fiber used for textiles.

WOOLLY FEATURES

Wool fibers are soft and stretchy. They absorb liquids like sweat and dyes well, and they can be washed clean and spring back into shape. These features make wool an excellent textile fiber.

Sheep are "dipped" regularly in a bath of strong chemicals to kill pests, such as fleas and lice, on their skin.

◀ *A sheep's woolly coat, or fleece, is cut off using scissorlike shears or electric clippers.*

WHAT IS WOOL?

Wool is similar to your hair and the fur of other animals. It is made of keratin, a protein substance. Each fiber grows from a tiny pit in the skin called a follicle. The main shaft of the fiber is made of millions of microscopic cells.

Rod-shaped cells of cortex (inner layer)

Flat, scaly cells of cuticle (outer layer)

WOOL FIBER

Alpacas have been sheared for wool for centuries.
▼

TYPES OF WOOL

The finest wool comes from the Merino and Rambouillet breeds of sheep. Other animals also produce wool-like fibers. These include camels in Africa and Asia and alpacas, vicuñas, and llamas in South America. Breeds of goats raised for wool include the Angora and Kashmiri. The finest wool comes from the undercoat, which is beneath the tough, coarse outer coat.

Uses of camelhair range from coats to tents.

Mohair is made from Angora goats' wool.

Medium fibers

4
3 5
6
8
1
7
12
2
Short,
coarse
fibers
9
11 10

Long,
soft, fine
fibers

Wool from different parts of the sheep has grades, from best (1) to worst (12)

IDEAS FOR THE FUTURE

Sheepshearing is a skilled and tiring job. In the future, we might have a new breed of sheep — the self-shearer! All of its wool would fall out when the sheep was fed a certain tablet. Like wool sheared off normally, the fleece would quickly grow back.

Sheep's wool soon grows back.

SILK

Silk is one some of the softest and smoothest, yet strongest, of all textiles. It has been produced and greatly valued since ancient times.

THE SILKWORM

Silk is different from other natural fibers made from animal products. It is not curly, wavy, or kinky. It is made from very long, smooth, thin filaments made by silkworms. Silkworms are not real worms. They are the caterpillars, or larvae, of a pale-winged, furry-bodied moth called the silk moth.

▲ *Silk moths have been bred in China for more than 4,000 years. Each adult female moth lays 500 to 700 eggs. A few cocoons from each batch are left so that adult silk moths can emerge and mate to make more caterpillars.*

A WORM'S LIFE

An adult silk moth (1) lays tiny, pale eggs. Each hatches into a small larva (2), which eats mulberry leaves (3) for five weeks. It spins a cocoon (4), and becomes an inactive pupa (5). Two weeks later the adult moth emerges.

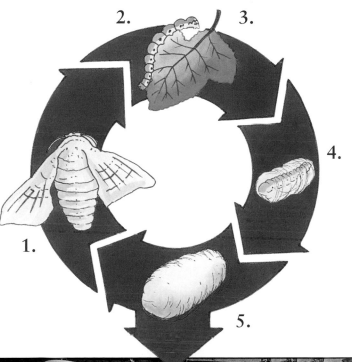

1.
2.
3.
4.
5.

The best silk is used to make very costly clothing. This ad from the 1920s also shows the silk moth and the caterpillar.

LONG, STRONG

A silkworm spins a single filament almost 5,000 feet (1,500 m) long for its cocoon. Cocoons are sorted into different grades of quality and softened in hot water. A filature machine combines several filaments into one thread of raw silk, which is wound onto a reel. Several threads may be spun together to make silk yarn thick enough for weaving.

Silkworms eat only fresh mulberry leaves (left). When they have spun their cocoons, the cocoons are collected and sorted (above).

Silk filaments are so thin that more than twenty may be wound and twisted to make a single piece of thread or yarn of raw silk.

CELLULOSE FIBERS

The first artificial, or man-made, fiber was produced in the 1880s. In fact, though this fiber was artificial, the substance it was made from was natural — wood!

RAYON

The artificial fiber known as rayon is based on cellulose, a material that is found in great quantities in wood. The wood is pulped and mixed with chemicals to obtain the cellulose, which is further treated and squirted through tiny holes to make long, smooth fibers.

This 1929 ad shows the silky qualities of rayon.

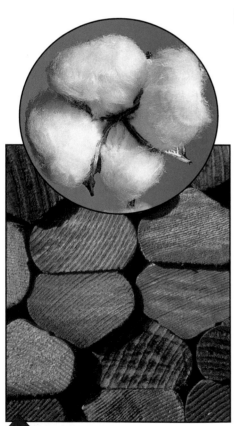

▲
Cellulose is one of the main substances in wood and in many other plant parts, such as cotton fibers.

MAKING RAYON

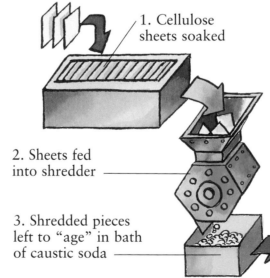

1. Cellulose sheets soaked

2. Sheets fed into shredder

3. Shredded pieces left to "age" in bath of caustic soda

4. Carbon disulphide added

5. Mix is churned into lumps

6. Mix dissolves to form pulp

Cellulose for rayon comes mainly from unwanted wood chips. The chips are soaked in a bath of chemicals to soften them and separate out the cellulose, which is pressed into sheets for the rayon process.

Viscose is made by mixing cellulose with caustic soda and carbon disulphide. Its fibers are ideal for making heavier fabrics. A similar process using copper oxide and ammonia produces finer filaments for silklike fabrics.

ARTIFICIAL SILK

The first types of rayon were invented as a more available and less costly form of silk. At first they were called "artificial silks." But in 1924, makers of the filaments agreed to call them rayon. Today, the various types of rayon make up about one-fifteenth of all artificial fibers. They have many uses, from elegant clothes to the strong, netlike webbing inside tires for cars, trucks, and motorcycles.

Rayon soaks up, or absorbs, liquids well. It is used for medical dressings and chemical filters.

The size of the spinneret's holes (below) affects the thickness of rayon filaments. They can also be stretched even thinner by jets of water.

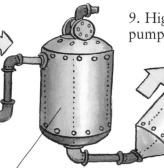

Rayon filaments are long, smooth, and straight, and they all have the same thickness.

IDEAS FOR THE FUTURE

Cellulose for rayon comes mainly from wood. In the future, a tree may grow cellulose fibers on the outside, like a stick of celery. These fibers could be used for rayon without cutting the tree down.

Celery has a fibrous outer layer.

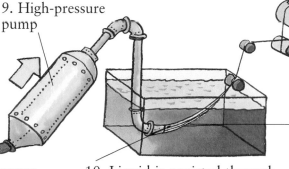

9. High-pressure pump

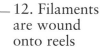
12. Filaments are wound onto reels

11. Filaments solidify in acid bath

7. Filter press turns mix into thick liquid

8. Settling tank removes air bubbles

10. Liquid is squirted through spinneret holes

ARTIFICIAL FIBERS

Following rayon (*see page 16*), scientists tried to make totally artificial fibers from mixtures of chemicals. They succeeded in 1938 — and have been making more new fibers ever since.

NYLON

The first fiber made completely from laboratory chemicals, rather than from natural substances, was nylon. It was an instant success, both for fashionable clothing and for military and industrial uses, such as parachutes and cords for strengthening tires. There are now dozens of artificial fibers. Many of these new fibers, such as polyester and acrylic, are types of plastics, made from petroleum.

Some of the substances refined from crude oil are used for making artificial fibers.

Clothing that looks natural may be made from artificial fibers.

Artificial aramid fibers do not rot in seawater.

Nylon begins with a mix of chemicals that include adipic acid and hexa-diamine. Heat and pressure cause a series of changes in the mix. As with rayon, nylon filaments are produced when the mix is squirted through a spinneret.

Nylon was successful for several reasons. It could be woven into thin, smooth, light, and strong fabrics that were easy to clean. Since it did not rot or get moldy, armed forces used it for tents, parachutes, and other gear. This quality is also why, starting in the 1960s, it became popular for carpets.

1. Mix is made stronger by evaporator

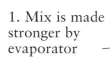

Computer

2. Oven heats mix to form nylon

3. Melted nylon oozes onto casting wheel and cools solid

Cooling water

4. Solid nylon is crushed into chips

5. Chips are mixed with hydrogen and melted

6. Liquid is forced through spinneret holes and cooled by air fan

Raw nylon mixture

7. Nylon fibers are spun and wound on spool

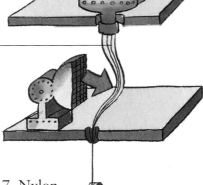

FACTS FROM THE PAST

Nylon was developed in the 1930s at the DuPont Chemical Company, by a team led by Wallace Carothers. He had the idea that molecules called monomers could be joined into larger molecules called polymers. These were long enough to form new fibers.

Wallace H. Carothers (1896–1937)

SPINNING

Natural fibers such as wool and cotton are too short to weave, sew, or knit. For this reason, these fibers are made into very long threads or yarns by spinning.

ROLL AND TWIST

The main idea in spinning is to twist together many short fibers so that they overlap each other and lock together with enough strength that they cannot slide past each other. Most cotton fibers are only around 3/4 to 1 1/4 inches (2 to 3 cm) long. At any place along a piece of cotton thread, almost one hundred fibers are tightly twisted together.

Before spinning, fibers such as cotton must be drawn (see below) several times. This process makes the fibers line up without bends, kinks, or knots.

CARDING

A natural fiber such as cotton is matted with unwanted bits and must be cleaned before spinning. In carding, the fibers are pulled past tiny wire hooks that comb

DRAWING

them into a strip, called the sliver. Next, slivers pass between rollers that draw them, or stretch them lengthwise and merge them into a strand, so their fibers run parallel.

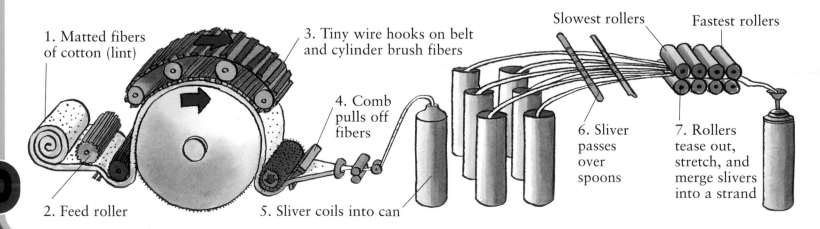

1. Matted fibers of cotton (lint)

3. Tiny wire hooks on belt and cylinder brush fibers

4. Comb pulls off fibers

2. Feed roller

5. Sliver coils into can

Slowest rollers

Fastest rollers

6. Sliver passes over spoons

7. Rollers tease out, stretch, and merge slivers into a strand

Until the 1200s, threads were hand spun using a whorl and spindle. In the 1300s, the spinning wheel greatly speeded up the job. In the 1700s, a series of spinning machines, among them the jenny, the frame, and the mule, were used.

A traditional spinning wheel being demonstrated

SPINNING BY AIR

The exact process of spinning depends on the types of fibers and their length, strength, and stretchiness. In open-ended spinning, blasts of air pull fibers into a fast-spinning cup and make them line up parallel as the cup twists them into yarn.

A spinning machine must wind the yarn or thread onto a reel, spool, or bobbin very neatly and at a very high speed.

ROVING

In roving, more rollers continue to stretch the strand. The strand then passes down the hollow arm of a spinning flyer and twists as it is fed onto a sliding bobbin. The first-stage

SPINNING

yarn, called roving, is again drawn so its fibers are parallel. Then they are fed through the traveler, a sliding loop, and twist naturally as they wind onto the bobbin.

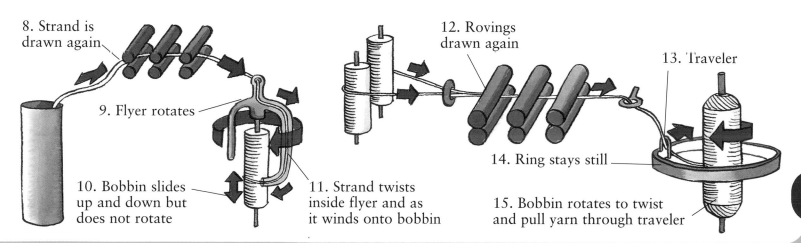

8. Strand is drawn again

9. Flyer rotates

10. Bobbin slides up and down but does not rotate

11. Strand twists inside flyer and as it winds onto bobbin

12. Rovings drawn again

13. Traveler

14. Ring stays still

15. Bobbin rotates to twist and pull yarn through traveler

WEAVING

The word "textile" comes from an ancient word that means "to weave." Weaving involves passing yarns over and under each other to form a piece of fabric.

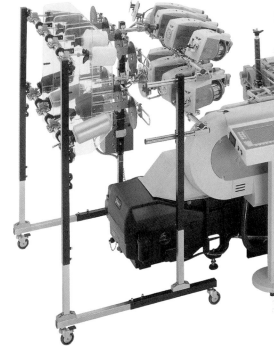

The Jacquard loom of 1805 used large cards with holes in them to produce woven patterns. It was an early automatic machine.

FIRST WEAVERS

Weaving was perhaps invented for making baskets and nets out of long vines and plant stems. In most textile weaving, one set of yarns is interlaced with another set by threading them under and over each other. This was once done by hand. Today, most weaving is done by machines called power looms.

WEAVING ON A LOOM

A loom has two sets of yarns or threads. Warp yarns lie lengthwise. The weft yarn feeds out of a small, pointed shuttle as it passes sideways between the warps. For one pass of the shuttle, frames or shafts lift even-numbered warps (2, 4, 6,...), while odd-numbered warps (1, 3, 5,...) are moved down. The process repeats, except with the warps reversed (evens down, odds up), so the weft can go the other way.

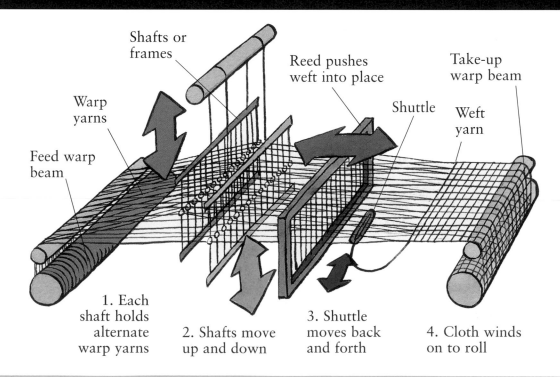

Shafts or frames

Warp yarns

Reed pushes weft into place

Take-up warp beam

Shuttle

Weft yarn

Feed warp beam

1. Each shaft holds alternate warp yarns

2. Shafts move up and down

3. Shuttle moves back and forth

4. Cloth winds on to roll

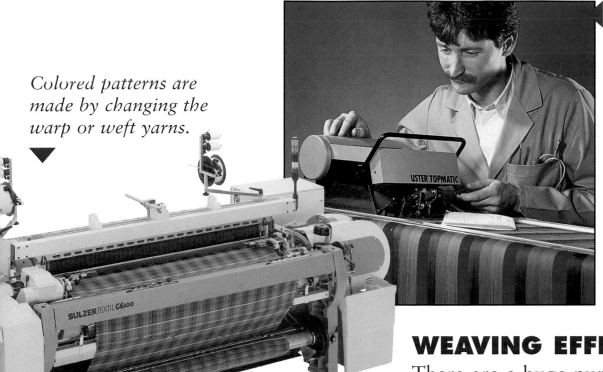

Colored patterns are made by changing the warp or weft yarns.

▼

For a smooth fabric, the warp and weft threads must be spaced evenly. They must also be pulled to the same tightness. The loom operator examines the cloth regularly and counts the number of warps and wefts in a certain distance to make sure the fabric is coming out well.

WEAVING EFFECTS

There are a huge number of different weave patterns. Thin yarns close together produce a close-weave fabric, while increasing the gaps makes for a more open weave. Bath towels have two sets of warp and weft threads. One makes the close-weave flat part of the cloth, the other forms the open-weave raised loops.

TYPES OF WEAVE

Plain weave: one warp for one weft

Twill weave: weft goes under two warps

Two thin warps with one thick weft

FACTS FROM THE PAST

Like spinning, weaving was once done by hand. Simple looms were in use in Europe and Asia about 5,000 years ago. Weaving became faster in 1733 when John Kay invented the "flying shuttle." This new shuttle was thrown quickly between the warp yarns by a device called a picker, unwinding weft yarn as it moved.

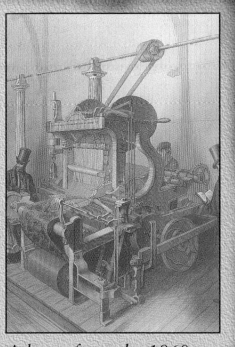

A loom from the 1860s

KNITTING, FELTING, AND MORE

At one time, the word "textile" meant only woven fabrics. Today, it also includes fabrics and cloth made by other methods.

KNITTING

In knitting, a long single length of yarn is used as both warp (lengthways) and weft (crossways). The knitter makes a series of knots, called stitches, by linking together loops of yarn using long, thin knitting needles or a machine. The pattern of knots makes the original length of yarn into a piece of fabric.

Knitting is one of the most common methods of fabric making. These machines can knit many different patterns.

IDEAS FOR THE FUTURE

Some substances are able to quickly take in heat and then give it out slowly. Could these substances be added to yarns of the future? In the future, you might be able to heat your coat before wearing it so it will warm you for hours in the cold.

Weft (purple)

Warp (green)

In a knit stitch, the loops are pulled to the front of the fabric (the side that shows). In a purl stitch (above), they are pulled to the back.

24

FELTING

A woven or knit textile has fibers and threads neatly arranged in patterns. A felted material does not. Its fibers are jumbled up at random. To make felt, the fibers are usually pressed hard and heated, perhaps with small amounts of gluelike chemicals, so they mat together with each other. Unlike woven cloth, which has lines and ridges, felts have the same texture in every direction.

Pool tables are covered by fine felt, while tennis balls have felt with thicker fibers.

Some textiles are treated to give them a "finish." Finishes are used for their appearance, to prevent creases or snags, or to make the fabric water-resistant. Singeing is a type of finishing in which fibers at the surface are slightly scorched. Napping is similar but uses tiny hooks to pull out some of the fibers. Luster uses chemicals and heat to create a smooth, shiny finish.

SINGE

NAP

LUSTER

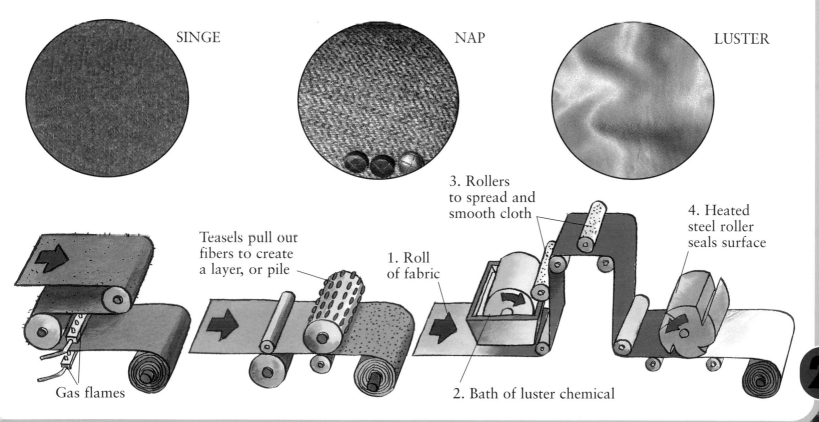

Teasels pull out fibers to create a layer, or pile

3. Rollers to spread and smooth cloth

4. Heated steel roller seals surface

1. Roll of fabric

Gas flames

2. Bath of luster chemical

DYES AND PRINTS

Some textiles are left untreated. They are the colors of their original fibers. But most textiles are colored in some way with dyes and prints.

PRINTING

Prints are pictures, words, and designs applied with colored inks to a finished garment, fabric, or other item. There are many methods of printing. Ink can be pressed onto the fabric from a wooden or metal block, or it can be applied by a revolving roller.

SCREEN PRINTING

In this type of printing, ink is pushed through tiny holes in a screen onto fabric. A mask stops ink from getting onto parts of the fabric where it is not wanted. As in most methods of printing, different colors of ink are applied separately, one after the other, to build up the complete picture or pattern.

Roller printing puts inks onto textiles very quickly.

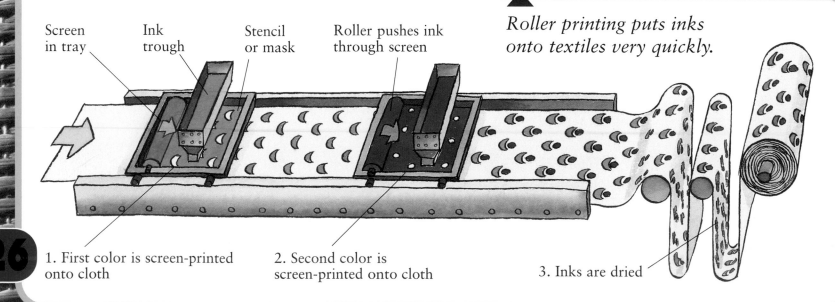

Screen in tray

Ink trough

Stencil or mask

Roller pushes ink through screen

1. First color is screen-printed onto cloth

2. Second color is screen-printed onto cloth

3. Inks are dried

DYEING

A dye is a strongly colored substance, or pigment, usually put in a liquid such as water. Textiles can be dyed at any stage — from the original fibers to the finished item — by soaking them in a vat with the dye. Different fibers, both natural and artificial, soak up and hold dyes in various ways. For example, rayon holds dye very well, but jute does not. Often yarns are dyed many different colors and then woven into a fabric in a certain order. This produces colored patterns, such as stripes.

William Perkin (1838–1907)

◀ *In tie-dyeing, fabric is tied with string so the dye cannot soak evenly into all parts.*

Iron-ons use special inks that soak into fabric when they are melted by heat from an iron. ▶

Carpetmakers weave very complex designs using many colors. ▶

27

TEXTILES FOR THE FUTURE

From original fibers to finished items, making textiles is a long and complex process. Many people, such as chemists who invent new kinds of artificial fibers and weaving experts who invent new ways of putting them together, are helping to develop new textiles.

There are more and more "breathable" fabrics such as Gore-Tex. They allow moisture to pass through one way only. When used for clothing, they let sweat from the skin get out, but they prevent wind and rain from coming in. They are excellent for outdoor and survival clothing.

Kevlar is used for bulletproof vests, almost unbreakable ropes, windsurfer sails, and hang glider wings. ▶

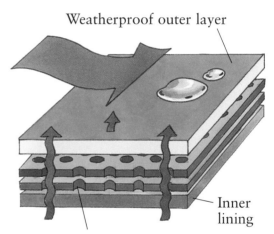

Weatherproof outer layer

Inner lining

Micropores (tiny holes) allow moisture to pass out, but not in

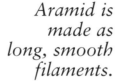

Aramid is made as long, smooth filaments.

STRONGER THAN STEEL

Some artificial or synthetic fibers are stronger than steel strands of the same size. Aramid has a chemical structure that is similar to nylon, but this fiber has even greater strength, and it resists heat and chemicals. It is woven into lightweight, ultra-tough, tearproof fabrics, such as Kevlar, which have many specialized uses.

RECYCLING TEXTILES

Clothes, curtains, carpets, and other items made from textiles cost millions to make, both in raw materials and in machinery and fuels. It is very important to reuse or recycle fabrics, especially by taking unwanted items to a clothing collection center. The fibers can be pulled apart and separated, and they can be used again to make felts, padding, cleaning pads, and similar products.

Clothes can be used again or processed into cleaning rags and other useful items.

COMBINING FIBERS

Most textiles are made by traditional spinning and weaving. But modern technology allows fabric designers to put together fibers in new ways, such as winding one type of fiber around another. New, stretchy materials have been made in this way.

Non-stretchy fabric

Stretchy fabric

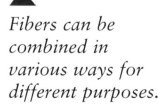

Fibers can be combined in various ways for different purposes.

Smooth, stretchy Lycra is ideal for sports clothing. ▶

TEXTILE CHART

	TYPE OF FIBER	FEATURES AND USES
ANIMAL	Wool (from sheep and other furry animals)	Very adaptable, springy fibers can be spun and woven in many ways, absorb moisture, keep in warmth; used for all kinds of clothes, blankets, carpets, insulation, and many other products
	Silk (from silkworm caterpillars)	Very long, smooth, thin, strong filaments; used for high-quality clothes, sheets, stockings, scarves, linings, tapestries
PLANT	Cotton (from seedpod or head of cotton plant)	Short, fluffy fibers spin and weave well, hold dye, absorb sweat and moisture, wash well, dry quickly; used for all kinds of clothing, underwear, bedding, towels, pads, medical items
	Flax (from stem)	Long, flexible fibers are not very stretchy; used to make sewing thread, nets, and twine, and woven into linen fabric for clothing, draperies, tablecloths, napkins, and other similar items
	Sisal or agave (from leaf)	Long, strong, stiff, coarse fibers; used for rough cloth, bags, ropes, string, and brushes
	Hemp (from stem)	Long, strong, stiff, long-lasting fibers; used for sacks, bags, rough canvas, ropes, and twine
	Abaca (from leaf stalk)	The strongest leaf fiber, also called Manila hemp; used mainly for "cordage" — rope, string, twine, cord, and cable
	Jute (from stem)	Very long fibers, but coarse, brittle, and difficult to dye; used for sacks, ropes, carpet backing, mats, and rough lining
ARTIFICIAL	Rayon/viscose (from plant cellulose)	Very long, smooth filaments, absorb moisture and dye well, adaptable in strength and softness; used for clothes, draperies, pads, filters, and reinforcing or strengthening webs and nets
	Nylon	Very long, smooth filaments, varied in strength and softness, resist dampness, rot, and chemicals; used for clothing, covers, draperies, ropes, string, fishing line, nets, and reinforcements
	Acrylic (propenoic acid, type of plastic)	Fibers can be made soft, fluffy, and "fleecy"; generally used in a similar way to wool
	Polyester	Hollow fibers are used for warm clothing, padding, and linings

GLOSSARY

cellulose: a substance that makes up large parts of plants, including wood, fibers, and the thick walls of microscopic plant cells.

dye: a colored substance, or pigment, usually spread out or dissolved in a liquid, such as water or a solvent, that is used to change the color of a thing that is soaked in it.

ginning: separating the fibers from the seeds and other parts of the cotton plant's boll (seed head).

polymer: a very large molecule (chemical grouping) made from many smaller units, called monomers, joined together.

retting: soaking parts of a plant so that they begin to rot and their fibers loosen.

shearing: clipping, snipping, or cutting the fleece from a sheep or other woolly animal.

spinneret: a nozzle with tiny holes through which liquid is squirted which then hardens into artificial filaments or fibers.

synthetic: artificial or man-made; something that is not found in nature.

warp: yarns or threads that lie lengthwise in a woven fabric, with the weft threaded sideways up and down between them.

weft: yarns or threads that lie crossways in a woven fabric, with the warp threads passing lengthwise up and down between them.

MORE BOOKS TO READ

Cotton Now & Then: Fabric-Making from Boll to Bolt. Karen B. Willing, Julie B. Dock, Sarah Morse (Now & Then)

Unraveling Fibers. Patricia A. Keeler, Francis X. McCall (Atheneum)

Wallace Carothers and the Story of DuPont Nylon. Unlocking the Secrets of Science series. Ann Gaines (Mitchell Lane Publishing)

What We Wear. Play & Discover series. Diane James, Sara Lynn (World Book, Inc.)

WEB SITES

Fabric Online – Textiles. *http://library.thinkquest.org./C004179/textiles.html*

Industrial Revolution – Textiles. *http://www.woodberry.org/acad/hist/irwww/Textiles/index.htm*

Due to the dynamic nature of the Internet, some web sites stay current longer than others. To find additional web sites, use a reliable search engine with one or more of the following keywords: *cotton, fabric, fibers, flax, Gore-Tex, jute, knitting, nylon, rayon, spinning, tie-dye, weaving.*

INDEX